Cats Rule!

Snap
books ®

Cat
SHOWS

Competing for Top Prize

by Rebecca Rissman

CAPSTONE PRESS
a capstone imprint

Snap Books are published by Capstone
1710 Roe Crest Drive, North Mankato, Minnesota 56003
www.mycapstone.com

Library of Congress Cataloging-in-Publication Data
Rissman, Rebecca, author.
  Cat shows : competing for top prize / by Rebecca Rissman.
    pages cm. — (Snap books. Cats rule!)
  Summary: "Describes cat shows, including the groups that organize them,
how they are run and judged, and how owners prepare for them"—Provided
by publisher.
  Includes bibliographical references and index.
  ISBN 978-1-4914-8401-2 (library binding)
  ISBN 978-1-4914-8413-5 (eBook PDF)
1. Cat shows—Juvenile literature. 2. Cats—Showing—Juvenile literature.
  I. Title.
  SF445.2.R57 2016
  636.8'0811—dc23   2015032923

Editorial Credits
Carrie Sheely and Alesha Halvorson, editors
Philippa Jenkins, designer
Svetlana Zhurkin, media researcher
Steve Walker, production specialist

Printed and bound in US

We would like to thank Laurie Patton, Regional Director, TICA Southeast, for
her invaluable help in the preparation of this book.

Photo Credits
Alamy: Gari Wyn Williams, 25, Steven Roe, 21; Capstone Press: Philippa
Jenkins, back cover and throughout; Dreamstime: Olga Volodina, 6; Granger,
NYC, 15; Newscom: Zuma Press/Greg Sorber, 27, Zuma Press/Michael
Holahan, 10; Shutterstock: Andrey Degtyaryov, 14, Anton Gvozdikov, 7, 8, 9,
26, Eric Isselee, 28, Konstantin Gushcha, 18, KWJPhotoArt, 5 (inset), Linn
Currie, cover, 5, 12, 17 (bottom), Lubava, 11, Marten_House, 19, photo_
master2000, 20, se media, 23, VGstockstudio, 17 (top), Ysbrand Cosijn, 13

Table of Contents

CHAPTER 1

Best in Show

In a busy convention center, a crowd gathers around a line of metal cat cages. Inside each cage is a beautiful cat.

It's almost time to compete! Quickly, you give Snowflake, your fluffy white Persian cat, one last brushing. Then you give him a little scratch behind the ears to calm him. Before you know it, a judge is carrying him to a table. You watch nervously as the judge feels Snowflake's face, body, legs, and tail. She looks carefully at his ears and eyes. You hope he behaves! Then just as suddenly as it began, it's over. The judge pets Snowflake and smiles before carrying him back to his cage.

The judge picks up a big blue **rosette**. She carries it to the line of cages and looks carefully at each cat. Then she carries it to Snowflake's cage and pins it to the bars. Everyone around you cheers. Snowflake has been named Best Champion. This award is given to the cat judged the best in its **breed**. Snowflake's first cat show is a success!

rosette—a ribbon award that is made to look like a rose
breed—a group of animals within a species that share the same features, such as color or markings

BEST OF SHOW

Persians are intelligent, which helps them adjust to being on a judging table.

CHAPTER 2

It's Neat to Compete

All around the world, from large cities to small towns, people gather to watch beautiful cats compete in shows. Cat shows are judged competitions. Cat owners enter their cats to compete for titles such as Best in Breed or Best in Show. They are exciting events for cat owners, cat breeders, and cat lovers alike.

Not all cat shows are the same. Some are small, local, and just for fun. Cats at these shows might compete in categories such as "funniest name" or "longest whiskers." Other shows are much larger. National shows attract breeders and owners who are serious about competition. There are even some international cat shows.

A cat remains calm while being judged at a show.

Cat breeding organizations sponsor some of the biggest cat shows. These organizations include the Cat Fanciers' Association (CFA), the Governing Council of the Cat Fancy, and The International Cat Association (TICA). One of the biggest cat shows is the CFA's International Cat Show. It's held in a different U.S. city each year.

Costs of Competing

Cat show registrations are usually between $50 and $75. Competitors may have to pay other fees for extra grooming space or a cage in a certain spot. They also need to take into account the money they spend on food, travel, and hotel fees.

A Big Event

Cat shows are busy places. Hundreds of cats
of different breeds, ages, colors, and genders
can compete in a single show. In addition to the
cats and their owners, there can be thousands of
spectators. Adding to the crowd are vendors selling
cat toys, collars, beds, and treats. Some cat shows
are even shown on TV.

People show their cats for different reasons.
Some people show **pedigree** or **purebred** cats.
Performing well at a cat show is a great way for
cat breeders to find new customers who might want
to buy their kittens. Other people participate in
cat shows just for fun. They enjoy meeting other cat
owners and seeing the show cats.

Thousands of people attend international competitions.

spectator—a person who watches an event
pedigree—having purebred ancestors
purebred—an animal that has been bred from parents and grandparents of the same breed

🐾 Head of Class

Cats competing in shows are divided into different **classes**. These are smaller groups of similar cats that are judged against one another. Depending on the number of competitors, the shows are typically one or two days long. Some common classes at major cat shows include championship, kitten, and veteran.

Championship Class

Cats in this class are eight months old or older, purebred, and have been **spayed** or **neutered**.

Premier Class or Alter Class

Cats in this class are eight months old or older, purebred, and have not been spayed or neutered.

Kitten Class

Cats in this class are purebred and between four and eight months old.

Veteran Class

Cats competing in this class are purebred and older than seven years.

Household Pet Class

Cats competing in this class are mainly non-pedigree or non-purebred, and have been spayed or neutered. Most competitions require that cats be at least eight months old to compete in this class.

Fanci Pantz (left), a Scottish Fold breed, shows off her ribbons at a cat show in Georgia.

Many cat owners choose not to declaw their cats.

Claws or No Claws?

In some countries, such as the United States, many owners declaw their cats. This surgery involves removing the last knuckle and claw from a cat's front paws. Not all shows allow declawed cats to compete. Many people have strong opinions about declawing. Some people believe it's cruel. They worry that a declawed cat can't defend itself if it becomes lost outdoors. They also feel that the surgery is painful and unnecessary.

class—a competition group of cats in a show
spay—to operate on a female animal so it is unable to produce young
neuter—to operate on a male animal so it is unable to produce young

Breeds and Rules

Cats in shows are often grouped according to their breed. Persian, Siamese, and Ragdoll are three common cat breeds. Different cat organizations recognize different numbers of official breeds. For example, TICA recognizes 63 breeds in its championship competitions. It recognizes another 12 in other smaller classes. The CFA recognizes 41 breeds in its championship competitions.

Cats of the same breed compete against one another. The winning cats from each breed then go on to compete in a show's higher levels.

Household cats are judged differently than purebred or pedigree cats. Judges score them on qualities such as personality, appearance, and uniqueness.

A Sphynx's personality is curious and energetic.

Did You Know?

Cat experts believe that the Egyptian Mau is one of the world's oldest cat breeds. These cats were first bred in ancient Egypt.

Bengal cats are the most commonly registered breed with TICA.

Both CFA and TICA record the number of cats registered in each breed. In 2015 the breeds with the most registered cats were:

Cat Fanciers' Association	
1	Exotic
2	Persian
3	Maine Coon
4	Ragdoll
5	British Shorthair

The International Cat Association	
1	Bengal
2	Ragdoll
3	Maine Coon
4	Persian
5	Sphynx

A proud tabby calmly sits at an international cat show in Moscow, Russia.

 Prizes

Cat show winners rarely earn money. Instead, they receive different colored ribbons. At higher levels of competition, the prizes are often large rosette ribbons. The winning cats and their owners also earn recognition. Breeders of winning cats can use these accomplishments to sell kittens to hopeful competitors.

Many people who compete in cat shows say that they are not interested in the awards. They participate because the shows are fun and a way to meet other people with similar interests.

🐾 Cat Show History

The world's first official cat show was held in Great Britain at London's Crystal Palace in 1871. Artist and writer Harrison Weir organized it. The show was a huge success. Organizers planned a follow-up show later that year.

a portrait of the prize cats drawn by Harrison Weir, the organizer of the first official cat show

CHAPTER 3

Getting Ready for the Show

Like any big event, shows require some planning. Good planning can reduce stress on competition day for both you and your cat.

Before entering their cats in a show, cat owners should attend at least one show as spectators. They can see how the competition is organized, how the cats are judged, and whether a show would be a good fit for their cats.

Getting the All-Clear

Owners also need to take their furry feline friends to their veterinarian for a checkup before shows. Cats must be healthy and have proof that they are up to date on vaccinations before they can enter a competition. Vaccinations help prevent a cat from getting sick with certain diseases. They help keep illnesses from spreading to other cats in the competition. Vaccinations can also help cat owners stay healthy.

Cats that will compete in a breed division must often be officially **registered**. Owners who register their cats usually need to provide proof of ancestry along with a small fee to a breed organization.

register—to enter something on an official list

Did You Know?

All cats should be checked and vaccinated for rabies. This illness can be deadly for cats and humans.

🐾 Cat Breeds

Cat breeds are created in different ways. The American Shorthair is a natural cat breed. It evolved over many generations to be strong, friendly, and grow a coat of short fur. Cat owners looking for certain traits created other breeds. Some breeds, such as the Persian and Turkish Angora, are hundreds of years old. Others are quite new. The LaPerm breed began in the United States in the 1980s. Cat breeders liked the cat's unique, curly coat. They bred cats that would pass on this trait.

The LaPerm can have a variety of coats, such as wavy or tight ringlet curls.

Show Supplies

Owners planning to show their cats will need a few supplies before a competition:

- Cat carrier: This large container keeps cats during travel. For safety reasons, always have your cat in a carrier when you travel.

- Carrier cover: These cloth covers fit over the cat carrier. They make the cat feel safe and secure inside the carrier. They also help block the cat's view of things that might frighten it, such as dogs or other people.

Grooming Supplies:

- cat combs and brushes

- facial tissue

- cotton balls and cotton swabs

- nail clippers

Different breeds may need different grooming supplies. Your veterinarian can recommend the best grooming supplies for your cat.

🐾 Practice Makes Perfect

Just like athletes before a big game, cats need to practice before a show. They need to become comfortable with travel, loud and busy places, and the experience of being judged.

Travel can easily overwhelm a cat. To get their cats used to travel, many show cat owners take their cats on short car trips. These trips get cats used to being in their carriers. Some cats are frightened or even become aggressive when they are put in their cat carriers. Practicing this task makes travel easier for both a cat and its owner.

Short car trips allow the owner to practice getting the cat in and out of the carrier.

Elegant cage drapes complement a cat's cage at a show in Birmingham, United Kingdom.

Cage Drapes

Cage drapes are decorative cloth curtains owners hang on their cats' cages at most shows. Owners often choose cage drapes that complement a cat's coloring or even highlight their cats' personalities. Some are fun and quirky, while others are classical and elegant. Some owners sew their cage drapes. Others buy them ready-made from specialty cat shops.

Dress Rehearsal

Owners can also prepare their cats by pretending to be cat show judges. This means placing the cats on tables or countertops and running their hands over the cats' faces, legs, bodies, and tails. The owner should look carefully at the cat's ears, eyes, and paws. After a cat is comfortable with this process, it's helpful for a friend or family member to pretend to be a judge. This exposes the cat to many people safely handling it.

Cat Scratch Fever

Cat scratch fever isn't a joke—it's real. And it can be very dangerous. If an infected cat scratches someone, the infection passes through the claws into the person's skin. People also can be infected if a cat bite breaks their skin or if a cat licks an open wound on their bodies. Cat scratch fever can make people very sick. That's one good reason to keep your cat's claws clipped.

Did You Know?

Cats who scratch or bite a judge or other official are usually disqualified immediately. This rule is for the safety of both the cats and human handlers.

Practicing with your cat mimics what the cat will experience at a show.

CHAPTER 4

Show Time!

The first morning of a major cat show is busy, exciting, and fun. The show hall is bustling with owners, cats, and cat lovers.

First, competitors check in and receive their cats' cage numbers and show numbers. The cage number tells the owner where to find his or her cat's cage. The cages are typically set up in long lines on display tables. The cage number often includes a row and aisle number. This helps both owners and spectators find cats. The show number is very important. This number is called when it's time for the cat to be judged. At some shows veterinarians examine the cats at check-in as well.

Cat cages are usually plain metal rectangles. Owners add their cats' bedding, food, water, and litterbox to the cages to make their cats feel comfortable.

Once they've set up the cages, most cat owners spend the last minutes before judging grooming their cats. This is the time for last-minute touch-ups, such as combing their cats' coats and clipping their claws one last time.

A cat rests in its cage during a competition in Rome, Italy.

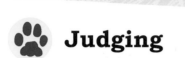

Judging

Cat show judges are trained for their jobs. They know the standards for each breed. Standards include traits such as head shape, tail length, coloring, and behavior.

At some shows owners must leave their cats in a separate judging area. The owners then pick up the cats when judging is done. At other shows owners can watch the judging along with the spectators.

A judge examines a cat's coat at an international event.

Did You Know?
For CFA shows, people who want to become show judges must have at least 10 years of cat breeding experience.

A judge engages with a Sphynx during the Enchanted Cat Club Show in Albuquerque, New Mexico.

When it is a cat's turn to be judged, a judge or assistant carries it to a judging table. There, the judge pets the cat, feeling for bone structure, coat quality, and build. The judges may take points off the cat's score for flaws or **defects**. These depend on the breed but may include a crooked jaw, crossed eyes, or a kink in the cat's tail. The judge also plays with the cat a bit to get a sense of its personality. Judging doesn't take very long. Usually the judge returns the cat to its cage within 30 to 60 seconds.

defect—a fault or flaw

The final level of
competition is often
called Best in Show.

The Winner!

At most shows cats earn awards in different levels of competition. During the first level, cats compete within their breed or class. The top-ranked cats then continue to higher levels of competition. The cat of any breed judged to be the very best cat in the competition receives the award of Best in Show.

Cat shows are known for their fun vibe and good-natured competition. The next time a cat show is in your town, grab your favorite cat-loving pal, and head over to take it all in.

How to Professionally Groom a Cat

Even if you won't be taking your cat to a show, you can make your cat look like a winner. If you've never groomed your cat, be very gentle and patient. Over time your cat will look forward to its grooming sessions. Remember that bathing and claw clipping are usually two-person jobs, so ask an adult to help you.

Step 1

Brush your cat's fur with a comb to remove any **mats** or loose hair.

Step 2

Place your cat in a tub or sink with a few inches of lukewarm water. Gently wet your cat. Rub cat shampoo into its fur. Rinse the soap from its coat. Gently dry your cat with a towel, and give it a treat as a reward. Many cats don't like being bathed, so be patient. And remember that while your cat should be brushed regularly, it only needs a bath before a show or if it gets too dirty to clean itself.

Step 3

Clip your cat's claws according to your vet's instructions.

Step 4

Once your cat is dry, brush it again. For shorthaired cats, use a metal comb and brush from head to tail. For longhaired cats, use a metal comb to brush the cat's body in an upward direction. Be sure to move your brush all the way down to the **undercoat**, but don't go down to the skin. If there are any mats in the fur, never try to cut it out yourself. A professional groomer will need to remove these. Finally, part the fur of the tail down the middle. Brush the fur out to each side. When you have detangled the tail, fluff it by brushing it upward.

Step 5

Using a cotton ball and rubbing alcohol, wipe out the inside of your cat's ears. Do not put anything into the cat's ear canal.

Step 6

Gently wipe the inner edges of your cat's eyes with a moist cotton ball. Wipe in a downward motion.

Step 7

Reward your cat with a treat and a scratch behind the ears.

mat—a thick, tangled mass of hair
undercoat—the short fur under a longhaired cat's outer coat

Glossary

breed (BREED)—a group of animals within a species that share the same features, such as color or markings

class (KLAS)—a competition group of cats in a show

defect (DEE-fekt)—a fault or flaw

mat (MAT)—a thick, tangled mass of hair

neuter (NOO-tur)—to operate on a male animal so it is unable to produce young

pedigree (PED-uh-gree)—having purebred ancestors

purebred (PYOOR-bred)—an animal that has been bred from parents and grandparents of the same breed

register (REJ-uh-stur)—to enter something on an official list

rosette (roh-ZET)—a ribbon award that is made to look like a rose

spay (SPAY)—to operate on a female animal so it is unable to produce young

spectator (SPEK-tay-tur)—a person who watches an event

undercoat (UHN-dur-koht)—the short fur under a longhaired cat's outer coat

Read More

Ganeri, Anita. *Kitty's Guide to Caring for Your Cat*. Pets' Guides. Chicago: Capstone Heinemann Library, 2013.

Hartman, Eve, and Wendy Meshbesher. *Animal Classification: Do Cats Have Family Trees?* Show Me Science. Chicago: Raintree, 2014.

Landau, Elaine. *Persians Are the Best!* The Best Cats Ever. Minneapolis: Lerner Publications Co., 2011.

Rau, Dana Meachen. *Kids Top 10 Pet Cats*. American Humane Association Top 10 Pets for Kids. Berkeley Heights, N.J.: Enslow Elementary, 2015.

Internet Sites

FactHound offers a safe, fun way to find Internet sites related to this book. All of the sites on FactHound have been researched by our staff.

Here's all you do:

Visit *www.facthound.com*

Type in this code: 9781491484012

Super-cool stuff! Check out projects, games and lots more at www.capstonekids.com

Critical Thinking Using the Common Core

1. What are some of the things you need to bring with you to a cat show? What are they used for? (Key Ideas and Details)

2. What are some things a judge looks for when interacting with a cat? What are some of the things that can earn a cat points? (Key Ideas and Details)

3. On pages 4–5, a cat is about to be awarded the Best Champion rosette. Imagine that you are that cat. What are you feeling? Write a short diary entry about your experiences at the cat show. (Craft and Structure)

Index